The Phenomenon of the Human Distress Pattern

Our Only Real Enemy

Written and Illustrated by Micheline Mason

WORKBOOK PRESS LLC
187 E Warm Springs Rd,
Suite B285, Las Vegas, NV 89119, USA

Website:	https://workbookpress.com/
Hotline:	1-888-818-4856
Email:	admin@workbookpress.com

Ordering Information:
Quantity sales. Special discounts are available on quantity purchases by corporations, associations, and others. For details, contact the publisher at the address above.

ISBN-13:	978-1-957618-10-4 (Paperback Version)
	978-1-957618-11-1 (Digital Version)

PUB.DATE: 05/10/2023

The Phenomenon of the Human Distress Pattern

Contents

Background

As a disabled child back in the 1950s I led a strangely isolated life. Until I was nearly 15, my life was mostly peopled by my Mum and Dad, my sister and a few hours of a Home Tutor every week. This gave my mind a lot of time to question, wonder, read and think for myself.

I noticed very early that well-meaning adults spoke a lot of nonsense, especially about me. My parents were told a lot of 'facts' which turned out to be just opinions, with no connection to reality. For example, doctors stood in their white coats and long faces and told my parents that I would die within weeks of being born. Obviously, they were wrong. The 'fact' of my imminent end was a painful memory held by a doctor who had been unable to save the life of a previous infant patient with a similar condition to my own. The mixture of lack of clinical information – why I was not the same as her – and his own unprocessed fear and grief had distorted his view of the current situation leading him to believe his gloomy prognosis. It took months for everyone to re-think their notions of my potential future, but by then a lot of harm had been done to me and my family. However, it was a good thing that we all learned that people, even The Professionals can be wrong about things. We had to learn to think critically and to recognise that finding the 'truth' is often a long search.

During my childhood I met many others, mostly adults, who had preconceived notions about people like me. They shouted at me as if I was deaf, spoke in simple words as though I couldn't understand things. Some didn't speak to me at all, preferring to speak about me instead to the more 'normal' looking adults who were with me, as if I wasn't really there. A radio programme of that era about disability-related issues was called "Does He Take Sugar?" in recognition of this bizarre behaviour.

I began to get the feeling that I had been born into a giant asylum full of people whose heads are full of misinformation and irrational emotions. Even my parents who actually knew me held some of these funny ideas. It was a matter of utmost importance to me that I found out why people were like this because otherwise, as they wielded such power over my life, they would clearly get in the way of my own inner drive to develop fully as the unique person I actually was. They would prevent me from having a life of my own. I knew even then that no one exactly like me had ever existed and therefore no one could prophesise what my future would be. This is true of everyone of course. We are all 'one-offs'.

When I was about seven I remember an image that came to mind as I was supposed to be listening to a very boring sermon from our priest. I saw a hand with clenched fist which then opened flat. Inside the hand was some sort of material which, like a piece of foam rubber, sprang out from its compressed ball within the iron grip of the fist into a large airy shape all uneven and interesting. It balanced perfectly on the support of the open palm. I thought then that this is what people are like, compressed by the hands of others, but able to spring back if released. I felt I was being compressed but somehow had the awareness that so was everyone else. 'I wonder what makes us do this to each other' I thought. 'And how can we stop doing it?'

Answering this question became a lifetime search. Much of this search went on inside my head. Like many young people, especially young women, I made friends with whom I sat up until the early hours trying to talk our way to an answer our own questions. We discussed endlessly why our friends had done this and that, to try and get a better understanding of their motives, especially when they had upset us. We did work out that past experiences affect current feelings and behaviours. We knew that this was true of ourselves and told each other snippets of our past lives. We laughed and cried over these memories and to some degree came to conclusions of our own.

A later experience moved me one step forwards. At the age of about 20 I invited myself to a residential event run by an unusual outfit called 'The Alternative Society'. I went as a craft-tutor, having taught myself the art of Batik all of a week beforehand. Evening brought about a quiet time when meals had been cooked and eaten, craft projects left to set or dry and discussions began.

I had not until that time met a diverse group of adults who were all questioning the 'Status Quo'. I found to my amazement a voice I didn't know I had. It seemed that the expressed thinking of other people gave me a new language with which I could talk about ideas I had, that had until that moment existed in my mind just below the level of consciousness. In that stimulating and non-judgemental atmosphere thoughts and insights came clattering out into the light of the shared space between us. They bounced off each other and changed shape. We left the room to wend our ways to bed sometimes too excited to sleep. We all left that gathering different people to those who had arrived.

Such 'safe' spaces to share and expand my thinking were hard to find. Many attempts to discuss things with other people were frustrating and tiring. Everyone seemed to want to use the attention of the other rather than actually listen without interruption. It was rare to even finish a thought before the conversation had been derailed by the other person grabbing the attention and to be fair, the pull to drag the conversation back to my agenda was also pretty overpowering. Because there is so little space to process our thinking with other people, it doesn't get processed.

Mostly though this is something we do not realise. We just notice as I had even as a young child, that many good and intelligent people talk varying amounts of rational sense, which can then flow seamlessly into nonsense, often with very strong emotions attached. I also noticed that we are usually unaware ourselves that we are going from one to the other. Consequently, our behaviour can be useful or can be guided by irrational thoughts without our knowing. Not much good usually comes of the latter. Sometimes great harm can come of it. My awareness of all this was unformed, sloshing around in my brain without the words to describe it, or the means to understand it. I was still searching.

Great fortune led my search to one of those exceptional minds, seemingly bigger than most, definitely bigger than mine. A public lecture by a 'Mr Frank' in 1975 suddenly handed me the information I needed. He offered an explanation to the cause of human irrationality. I was excited. To me it did not feel like new information. It felt more like a revelation of my own hidden understandings and beliefs and as such I felt it was right.

'Mr Frank' was not just offering a theory however. He was offering a safe space in which to experience all these things for ourselves. The point of that was not to pass an exam or simply understand the hopelessness of the human condition, it was to **reclaim our minds for ourselves and each other.** 'Mr Frank' believed that if we could release ourselves from the phenomena of the human distress pattern we would be capable of building a rational society based on answering real human needs.

I wanted to learn all I could about releasing people from the 'compressing' forces I had pictured back in my childhood and joined his organisation as a student. There I learned for myself about the phenomena of the human distress pattern, then practiced, applied it to myself, and taught to others to do the same for over 40 years. I experienced this organisation as a 'crucible' where many thousands of people, in many different countries, came together in pairs or groups to experience and refine the underlying theory which gradually emerged in an extraordinary 'experiment' aimed at uncovering our true human potential. Hopefully I made my own contribution to this. *(For reasons of confidentiality I have changed the name of it and its' leaders).*

After 'Mr Frank' died, I felt a pressing need to give back to the world the precious information he had given us. I want to share and make accessible his gift, especially to working class people who have so little space to think for ourselves. This is the purpose of this little book.

Part One:

The Theft of Our Minds

Our basic Human Nature

A human being has possibly the most complex brain of all living creatures. We are capable of growing millions of neural pathways along which limitless information can ebb and flow. We have at least five senses through which we collect data from the moment of conception to the moment of death, and it seems possible that our brains retain it all, like the biggest computer in the world. A smell can lead us back to memories of that smell – frying bacon, a musty classroom, some ones' perfume – and all the feelings and activities associated with it.

There is so much stored data that most of it is tucked away beneath our conscious attention otherwise we would just mentally drown in chaos, a human land-fill dump. But we don't. Instead it is the nature of our brains to sort and store everything for later use just like our sock drawer, matching pairs and rolling them together then closing the drawer and thinking about something else until it is time to choose a fresh pair of socks. This is an amazing capacity, so what is the problem?

We Get Hurt

Unlike a computer, or a sock drawer, we have emotions. These emotions release chemicals in the form of hormones into our bloodstreams and consequently our brains, such as serotonin which is released when we are experiencing 'happiness' or cortisol which is released when we are afraid or 'stressed'. This is a naturally occurring phenomena which is meant to help us seek out useful, life-enhancing experiences such as a nice dinner or a warm hug, and avoid dangerous or damaging experiences such as being eaten alive by a hungry bear. These floods of specialized chemicals have the effect of temporarily halting the normal functioning of our thinking processes in order to focus our attention on the immediate danger or threat.

Everyone of us can recall times when something awful happened – a car hit ours maybe – and we felt we could no longer think, we were 'beside ourselves'? Automatic responses take over – we shake with fear, shout for help and so on. Gradually we start to think again and we work out what to do. Inside our heads the flood of chemicals starts to subside until they reach normal levels again. But herein lies the problem. In general, we have not noticed that the crying, the shaking, the rapid talking is all a natural process of our brains which helps the chemical levels to subside. Even laughing is a spontaneous response to uncomfortable experiences such as embarrassment or confusion.

We do know all these things make us feel better but we don't know why or recognize how essential they are to our ability to think rationally. Consequently, we have created a culture in which we have a very limited tolerance of these purely emotional processes. When babies cry our usual reaction is to shove something in their mouths as quickly as possible – a nipple, a teat, a dummy – anything to stop that noise. We continue this throughout childhood with distractions, threats, put-downs and even violence. The same goes for too much talking, laughing, and tantrums. The last thing we are taught to do is to encourage them but this is the biggest mistake we humans make. **What we are doing without realizing it is forcing our minds to create distress patterns, and these patterns are the cause of human irrationality. These patterns are our only real enemy, not the people who have them.**

The mind is 'hard-wired' to bring our levels of chemicals to levels in which our natural intelligence can function (sorting the sock drawer). In order to do that we need to engage in the process of emotional expression which itself alters, or restores our natural chemical balances. If we are prevented from using this process, our memory of the painful event freezes into an 'ice-ball' with all the information that was coming in at the time through the senses – all the sounds, smells, sights and feelings you had at the time - unsorted and intact. Because our minds are driven towards restoration, it stores this ice-ball in a special place all ready to try again at the process, if the opportunity should ever arise.

In effect this means we have inside us two different stores of information. One is like our sock drawer, which we can open and close at will, using the socks inside as and when we need them, *and* a store of emotionally 'charged' memories which are more like recordings inside a malevolent tape recorder. When the button is pushed on this machine we are compelled to re-experience the hurtful memory as if it is happening again in the present and with it comes the inability to think properly as happened the first time. Our behaviour consequently relates to something that happened in the past, not the current reality, but there is always the hope that someone will listen to us whilst we enact the healing process we should have done back then.

The Need for Attention

Here lies the rub. When as an infant we cry for our mothers to feed and comfort us there seems to be a natural expectation that someone will come to our aid. We are not designed to live alone but in communities of interdependence. *We need the attention of someone else to survive.*

The other big thing we don't notice or understand is that we are not only 'hard-wired' to need attention, we are 'hard-wired' to give it too. Maybe most new parents are aware of their delight in tending to their new little bundles of joy, but this instinct is hardly supported by the societies we have created, especially the so-called 'developed' ones. It's Back to Work as soon as possible. None of us grow up psychologically or emotionally intact as a consequence. It is a matter of luck as to the degree of damage we are living with, or the amount of flexible intelligence we can draw upon. The fact that everyone has frozen ice-balls driving us to think and behave in irrational ways is the biggest threat to our survival we face.

There is no limit to the things our distress patterns will drive us to do. We will kill each other and ourselves. We will rape and torture, we will steal, plunder and exploit. Because the nature of our distress pattern usually conjures up early feelings of victimhood and powerlessness, at the time of carrying out these actions we can think we are justified in doing so in the name of self-defence, or revenge. People in the grip of their patterns are nearly always unaware of the real effects of their behaviours in the here and now.

People not in the grip of their patterns have unlimited scope for altruism, courage and self-sacrifice. What is utterly confusing to many of us is the evidence that both kinds of behaviours can be displayed by the **same person.** We have all heard stories of Nazis who spent hours each day burning Jews and others in gas ovens, and then going home and tenderly reading a bed-time story to their little children. All explanations based on notions of good people (like us) and bad people (like them) do not really hold water when the whole picture is seen.

Our Basic Drives

There is no evidence that I know to show that babies are born good or bad. There is evidence though to suggest at least that we are born with common needs and common drives. We are like seeds that clamour to grow to their full size as is genetically programmed and set in their DNA. An acorn really does strive to become an oak tree, able to grow acorns of its' own. Humans strive to become fully developed in every way possible. It may be our only real purpose, to 'become'.

Because we need the care and attention of others to do this it seems our fundamental nature is co-operative.

Because we have always known that we are dependent on the abundance of nature, it seems that whilst meeting our own need for food, for example by hunting and gathering, all early peoples revered plants and animals, and protected the ability of natural resources to regenerate themselves.

Because we need as much information as possible in order to develop all our skills and potential we seem intensely curious and wanting to learn from day one (maybe before) not just 'facts' but through experiences. Almost all children want to get their hands on everything and have a go at everything from morning to night.

As well as plenty of opportunities to explore the world, the experiences gathered need processing in order for it to be stored away in the sock drawers of our minds, and this often requires the attention of other people, to answer our questions and listen to us working things out.

Because we need to feel safe and secure in order to put attention to our own development it seems that we expect our 'carers' to provide that security so we can get on with it, especially when we are children. Likewise, most adults are strongly motivated to provide security, physical and emotional to their families and other close ones. It is mutually beneficial and safeguards our survival as a species.

You could call all these the elements of our 'basic human nature'. If any of these needs are not met it is experienced as stressful. In response stress hormones are produced and a resolution is sought. Either the need gets met through someone responding to the call for help, or a little ice-ball starts to form.   Later we may find the attention we need to melt the ice-ball, releasing the 'data' into our drawers, or maybe we won't.

Ice-balls in our minds

The Formation of Ice-balls (Patterns)

The bad news is that each time an event happens similar enough to the first one and we fail to get the attention we need to melt the ice-ball, it grows. It grows bigger and bigger, adding to it the new disappointment of not getting the help needed.

Because our brains have a massive capacity, especially when we are young and our brains are still growing, we can have a lot of ice-balls standing around without our really noticing, but if the stressful events keep on happening, e.g. not enough to eat every day, the ice-ball can become a monster, even fooling the person into believing they are still hungry even when stuffed with dinner. The tape recorder in our heads is permanently switched on, altering our sense of reality. In this way we are all a bit mad, not just some of us.

Permanent Ice-balls (Chronic Patterns)

As well as intermittent patterns which only get switched on – restimulated – when something reminds us enough of the first time we experienced a particular distress, we have chronic patterns. These are recordings that have been restimulated so often the start button is jammed in the 'on' position and they play all the time. They are much worse than the first kind because they come to feel so real that we believe they are us. "I was born shy", "I am not very bright", "I can't draw", and they obscure reality from us "No-one can be trusted", "I am ugly", "I cannot do anything about it" etc.

All this is of far more importance than individual misery or personal limitations.   Patterns are responsible for nearly all the destructive behaviours which harm each other, and are now threatening the natural balance of life on earth. Patterns drive individuals to suicide and they could be driving the whole human race to self-destruction.

Some would say that 'greed' is the fundamental human problem and it is easy to see why with 1% of people 'owning' the majority of the wealth and power in the world. But a few psychologists, such as Oliver James ('Affluenza' 2007) have studied the motives behind such apparent greed and found that everyone, however much they had, truly felt they needed half as much again to feel 'safe'. Fear was driving them, and an unfillable need to feel they had enough.

Frozen Needs

A frozen need is feeling in the present a rational need which was unmet in our childhoods.

If for example we suffered hunger as a child it is possible that a feeling of hunger will be triggered at all meal times, driving us to eat too much. We will be addicted to food. Because this feeling is a past recording and not a current reality it will not go away however many doughnuts we stuff in our mouths. Not much later we will be hungry again. The memory is frozen in the ice-ball and the real need for food become frozen too and as such cannot be met until we melt the ice-ball, dissolving the craving into just a memory belonging to the past.

Trying to fill 'Frozen Needs' is one of the strongest drives we have. The futile nature of this endless search wastes more of our time than anything else, sometime hi-jacking our whole lives. The search for love and affection, attention and respect are probably almost universal in our current societies because very few children get enough.

When looking for romance we are usually hoping that within this deep and exclusive relationship we will find the attention needed to get on with our ice-ball melting mission, especially these damned frozen needs. The safer we feel with someone the braver we become about showing them our personal struggles, or patterns, with the hope that they have a clear enough picture of our real selves that they will help us do the melting by their warmth, encouragement, validation and time to offer a literal shoulder to cry on.

Sometimes this does happen and the relationship is truly healing, especially when it is a reciprocal giving and taking of attention. However, given that most of us don't really understand this process, it can often go wrong. We may keep our worst behaviours for those with whom we feel the safest, acting out our 'recordings' unawarely and repeatedly. This can include all sorts of abusive words and actions including sexual and physical violence.

Our partners, all with their own burden of ice-balls, will understandably feel hurt, attacked and 're-stimulated', re-activating all sorts of defence mechanism and retaliations which only make matters worse. I would suggest this is why two out of every three marriages (in the UK) end in divorce.

Patterns are an explanation for addictive behaviours of all kinds. Anything locked into an 'ice-ball' and forced to replay itself repeatedly will look like and feel like an addiction because of its repetitive nature.

The Systemic Freezer

We all have far more in common than we have differences. In fact, we are all virtually the same - we are all one human race, yet it would appear that those with most power in the world do not want us to realise this. It appears to suit their ends to convince us otherwise.

We are divided by our social class, our gender, our ethnicities, our abilities, our age, our political leanings and much more. Each group is further sub—divided into smaller groups. Our family for example identified ourselves as 'Upper Working Class' because we pronounced our words properly, saying 'think' and not 'fink' showing that we were not 'common' like that awful family down the road.

Eventually we each feel we belong to a tiny group, different to all others and therefore a minority without power, competing for scarce resources with all others. All this has been achieved by a multitude of individual hurts. These hurts are so widespread that they can distort our understanding of human nature, masquerading as 'normality' when in fact they are more like a manufactured glacier, making us feel cold and icy towards people who are appear different to us, instead of kind and empathetic as is our nature.

Oppression

We are all steeped with the effects of living in an oppressive society and there is a mountain of information about it, but there are still some key issues which are rarely included in the catalogue of misinformation we need to address as a whole world population.

First and foremost is **Classism** - the fundamental economic oppression which evolved to justify a massive inequality of resources and power in the world. We have to believe each group deserves their place in the hierarchy because of their inborn differences of intelligence or morality or we wouldn't put up with it. How we come to hold these beliefs can only be explained by the hurts we suffer as we grow up which are far more than we generally realise.

Racism – the false belief that there is more than one race of people and some races are superior to others because of inherited and fixed genetic differences. At its' worst racist beliefs would consider some people 'sub-human'. This has been used to justify slavery, antisemitism, islamophobia and genocide. Conversely it has been used to justify the exultation of royalty, posh people in general, and white-supremacists.

All the information spread about to convince us that these differing values placed upon human beings is natural and inevitable was conceived of, and published by, the white owning class. They invented a whole pseudo-science called 'Eugenics' to justify their privileged positions.

Their aim was to prove that the inferiority of poor people, women, black people and people with impairments was the inevitable result of their genes, which couldn't be changed. IQ was deemed to be fixed and inherited. Their duty therefore was to protect their own bloodline by isolation and in-breeding (including marrying their own cousins) and limiting the reproduction of people with 'lesser' genetic endowment through birth-control (for working-class women), enforced sterilization and incarceration in single-sex institutions of all manner of 'deviants' to prevent them breeding and thus weakening the nations gene pool. *(See 'Silenced – the Hidden History of Disabled Britain' BBC 2, 2021).* Even though many of the 'facts' in their theories have been shown not to be true, many people are still profoundly confused by them.

Racism is used all over the world to divide working people from each other, pitting us against each other instead of our real oppressors.

The third key oppression is **Adultism.** All children everywhere in the world and into whatever social class or caste they are born, suffer oppression, having few, if any, rights of their own before they (we) legally become adults.

It is vital to understand that both victims and perpetrators need to be hurt as children if they are to accept their pre-ordained roles in adult life. If like me you had been bought up to think that the people who 'perpetrate' oppression do so because they are wicked and enjoy making other people suffer, or that they feel safe and powerful in their exalted positions, the opportunity to be allowed behind the masks and to hear about the 'grooming' process they were forced through as children changed my understanding completely. Within the 'Crucible' I met and got close to people from the British Owning Class, the inventors of capitalism and its two-class system.

One story I remember vividly is of a little owning-class boy burning his parent's money and throwing his mothers' jewellery all around the local woods. Both the police and a child psychiatrist were called in. He told me how he and his siblings had to line up every day outside his Fathers office and 'account for themselves'. If their day's activities did not meet with his approval they got beaten. He told me of sexual abuse at his Public School and how it left him too distressed to study. Many other people from this class told stories of being deprived of parental love and affection, with their nannies and childminders bringing their only experience of kindness. One woman talked lovingly of a tree on the long branches of which she used to lie naked for comfort.

It is not hard to work out that such enduring profound unmet needs whilst at the *same time* being told you are one of the lucky ones, one of the privileged, is deeply emotionally confusing. Generations of being groomed to be our rulers whilst being consistently left wanting what in fact much poorer people (like me) had in bucketsful, has created a world leadership of very damaged and dangerous people. They are driven by their patterns, their 'frozen needs', created by the patterns of generations before them. They will never believe they have 'enough'.

Many people from these backgrounds, to my surprise, were deeply envious of my family life, full of affection and laughter despite the damp walls and lack of money. When I stopped feeling a victim in relation to these people and their gated communities, I started to see things differently. They were as much victims of their social 'position' as all the rest of us. I stopped hating them (mostly) and directed my attention to finding out how to help them reclaim their humanity.

For the majority of people to accept systematic inequality we have to be hurt, ice-balls need to be created, and our abilities to think and act severely constrained. This is as true of the Owning Class, the Middle Class and the Working Class worldwide.

There are many forms of oppression and recently a new word – 'intersectionality' - has become popular. It acknowledges that the same person can be affected by more than one oppression - race, class and gender for example. The burden of mistreatment on a black disabled woman will be heavier, like adding more layers of bricks in a wall, than on a white able-bodied woman for example, although both will be hurt by sexism.

Internalised Oppression

Internalised Oppression is a term which refers to the way in which we come to believe the negative messages we are given about ourselves as oppressed people. These feelings can exist within us even when we are no longer being directly oppressed. As a disabled girl for example, I was told that only my own family would love me. Over 70 years later and despite much evidence to the contrary, I can still doubt that I am loveable.

Worse still, not only do we harbour negative feeling about ourselves, we harbour them about our whole group, or groups. For example, it is not uncommon for working class people to feel middle-class people in general are more clever, refined and capable of leading than themselves.

This internalised self-doubt affects all oppressed groups. I recall Nelson Mandela in his autobiographical book 'Long Road to Freedom' describing his consternation when he saw that the pilot of the plane he was boarding was black. He wanted to get off. He didn't trust him to fly the plane safely as would the more usual white pilots. That was internalised oppression.

'Mr Frank' believed that without our internalized oppression we would not accept oppression in general and within the 'Crucible' we worked hard to melt these particular ice-balls. As other people's internalised oppression is much easier to recognise than our own, the fact that we can deliberately decide to help each other to become free of these 'chains' by the deliberate exchange of attention was, and is, hugely hopeful.

State Reinforcement

As well as the hurts of oppression, our minds are under attack from supplementary systems which reinforce the misinformation. One system of particular relevance to this book and its' proposition is our Mental Health System:

The Mental Health System

When our needs are not met it causes us great distress. Medicalising social needs is a form of 'blaming the victim' which perpetuates the underlying problem of inequality.

Our great big mental health system makes a heap of money by persuading us that our strong feelings are signs of illness requiring expensive therapies and drugs delivered by well-paid professionals and multi-dollar pharmaceutical companies. At the same time, they will mostly sheepishly admit that there is precious little evidence of 'disease' in the physical organ called the brain of people who are diagnosed with a wide range of mental 'disorders' from Depression to Schizophrenia. I do not feel 'qualified' to say that there is no such thing as mental illness, but it is self-evident that if normal people's rational needs are not met, this causes stress and affects our feelings and behaviours.

The delicate balance of chemical messengers in our heads, with its self-regulating systems can be upset, damaged, and even rendered unable to operate by the use of drugs. This includes 'recreational' drugs such as alcohol or cannabis as well as medicinal drugs. A 'recording' or pattern first formed by an event which caused our brain to create a flood of hormones – adrenalin for example, to help us have the extra energy to run away from a perceived danger will be locked in the 'Ice-ball', creating a new flood every time it is 'triggered, or restimulated', therefore chemical imbalances can occur repeatedly if that is an unhealed hurt we carry around with us. Trying to redress the balance by administering different chemicals can appear to improve our behaviours and even thinking, but unfortunately, they can also block the natural healing process from working. The ice-block doesn't melt and symptoms can keep coming back whenever life reminds us enough of the original stress or trauma.

If we are lucky enough to find better ways to deal with these feelings, we are capable of deciding not to use unnecessary drugs anymore. I have known long-term patients who were able to stop using psychiatric drugs and stay well through the process of identifying and 'discharging' or 'melting' deep early hurts.

Less controversially, it is one of the most remarkable features of a long-term commitment to using the process of peer-counselling within the 'Crucible' that most of its many thousands of members voluntarily gave up smoking and drinking alcohol. It wasn't a requirement, unless you wanted to be authorised to teach classes on its underlying theory, but mostly people did, including me, and most continue not to smoke or drink for the rest of their lives even if we/they leave the community itself. We like having our brains back, un-fogged by unnecessary chemicals.

The State Education System

We have an inborn inner drive to learn through play, experimentation and practice. We are always absorbing information of interest to us. Watch any young child busying herself from morning to night to be reminded.

The way learning is organised in general through our State Education System is more one of enforced delivery of information from Teacher to child whether they are interested or not. The curriculum is not the child's but the State's. This is reinforced by a whole battery of testing, ranking, notions of success or failure which are imposed on teachers and schools as well as children. As such it is a hurt. Because it is a hurt, through this system **we become more knowledgeable but less intelligent.** We may be more able to regurgitate information and pass exams, but the price we are paying is half a frozen brain, struggling to identify or work towards our own goals.

The System has another major function. Whilst we are born into a system already divided amongst class lines, it is at school that a new contingent of middle-class people are recruited from within the working-class. This is by selection (through setting and exams) and certain privileges. They are then shepherded off to university where they are further groomed to join the managers of the system – agents of the owning class. This separation is a hurt to both groups as it is divisive and reinforces the devaluing of certain kinds of skills and abilities, often referred to as vocational versus academic. This 'first generation' or 'Upwardly Mobile' group of middle-class recruits have to keep up the appearance of superiority for ever more however much they feel imposters.

As the middle-classes progress through the system, they often gain professional status and with it comes increasing access to resources and increasing power over the lives of working-class people. Not surprisingly those they left behind often harbour feelings of mistrust and resentment towards them.

To set it all in stone, the actual owning class have their own separate schools where they are never allowed to be part of ordinary life or make real contact with the people upon whom they inflict this system. This is a bigger hurt than most people realise as it often disguises how their own basic needs are not met, especially as children.

All of our current systems can be part of the reinforcement of the oppressive society despite the good people working in them who often do a great deal to try and 'humanise' them. Indeed, if this were not true the current systems would not work at all.

No systems or services can work if we continue to put people in situations where our needs are not met. This can only be 'cured' by changing our environment to one in which we can be healthy and flourish.

Segregation

Segregation and forms of apartheid have been used all over the world to maintain the oppressive society.

Disabled people like me have been victims of segregation through political, religious and fear-based theories ever since we created 'Civilisations'. The most current driver in the West has been the birth of capitalism. When the landowners forced the population off the land into factories and towns, the system of family wages which included disabled members, became obsolete. It was replaced by individual workers competing for a wage, and disabled people often couldn't do it.

The segregation of 'non-productive people' into asylums and other institutions is echoed in all kinds of enforced separations. These are often based on class, gender, race or religious lines but included the owning class themselves with their palaces, public schools and coming out balls. 'Eugenics' was designed and used to convince those who must fund it – The Church, voluntary organisations and tax-payers – that is was just a case of 'natural Selection' and a form of kindness.

Segregation is one of the most effective tools of the oppressive society because it breaks the relationships between people, preventing them learning about or caring for people different to themselves. Once separated all kinds of misinformation can be taught about the 'others' and mass stereotyping becomes unchallenged. The result is that most of us live in insular worlds where we do not have close contact to people outside of our own class, religious upbringings, abilities, nationalities or even political leanings.

Much of my adult life has been spent fighting against segregation and for inclusion. We have to know each other before we can plan a better world.

Glaciers within Society

There are many hurts we have in common, living as we do on the same planet, under the same systems and sharing the same misunderstandings of our human nature. Obviously, these are harder to spot as we are led to believe they are part of our normality and there are very few examples of people who don't have them.

Sexuality – What is 'normal'?

All of our strongest survival instincts are able to become distorted by mistreatment into a distress recording. The need for food, comfort, love and affection, and our natural 'animal; instinct to reproduce are fertile ground for exploitation by others – individuals and society as a whole.

Feelings of sexual attraction are perhaps the most insidious of all these vulnerabilities to distress recordings. We now have such a history of exploiting them that we are very unclear as to what is 'normal' in this area. The sexual attraction triggered in men by women's bodies is thought to be natural, but mostly it is a distress recording. The feelings are unbidden, triggered by a certain shape bottom or glimpse of cleavage for example, and many men confess to being tormented on a daily basis by having to drag their attention out of this distracting restimulation, especially in the Summer when more of these 'triggers' are exposed to the sunlight and their eyes. This obviously also applies to women's attraction to muscular bodies and broad shoulders in men etc.

Like all patterns they can become chronic and hi-jack someone's life.

The feelings of need can be so strong and the unawareness that they are not 'real' can lead to them becoming the dominant 'drive' in many people's lives. Given that other patterns, especially the desire to exploit our vulnerabilities in order to profit from them are also dominant in our lives, the toxic combination has led to a society which tells us this is all normal human behaviour and reinforces it at every opportunity.

Even the feelings of 'Falling in Love' should be viewed with suspicion. Most of us experience these feelings as a sort of madness "I am mad about you", with slightly obsessive, overpowering longing for the attention of a particular person often accompanied by strong sexual attraction. We are all of us to varying degrees led to believe that attaching these feelings to the right person will lead to 'Living Happily Ever after'. The multitude of evidence to show that it often fades, disappoints or turns into the opposite sort of feeling does not seem to deter us from pursuing this 'dream'.

Many of these chronic recordings can be much less benign than this. There is a continuum of examples from the relatively harmless recording which make a man feel 'turned-on' by dressing up in women's clothing, to the deeply harmful recording which lead to paedophilia, rape and even murder. Most women, despite our 'Reclaim the Night' marches, are still afraid to go out alone in the dark, for fear of becoming a victim of men's sexual distress patterns. We must never accept this as normal.

Of course, there are vast profits to made out of these distresses – the fashion industry, plastic surgery, pornography, and the sex industry to name but a few.

Addictions

There are many multi-million-pound industries set up to install patterns around these aspects of our humanity and then profit from them. 'The Men Who Made Us Fat' was a brilliant television documentary (2012) by Jacques Peretti on the exploitation of our need to eat and the natural pleasure we get from doing so. He then went on to make a second documentary 'The Men Who Made Us Thin' looking at the vast empire of slimming products, exercise bikes and so on to help us lose the weight the first industries had encouraged.

Food is just one of any number of addictions which can be manufactured, frozen into place by distress, and from which a new market can then be created to try to help us both fill them, and overcome them. For example, addiction to video games and other online activities is a rapidly growing threat to the mental health of young people, but which make millions in profits for the businesses concerned.

Chemical Dependencies

It is considered normal within our societies to use artificial drugs to manage our feelings. Getting drunk, smoking weed, swallowing anti-depressants and getting high at parties and gigs are things nearly everyone of us does at some time or other. We all buy them and some of us sell them, again making vast profits for the corporations who produce them. Even food can be a chemical cosh, a 'comfort' which we use to dampen our uncomfortable feelings. It is hard to imagine current societies functioning if we didn't. All our upsets would rise up and demand to be heard instead of 'Keeping Calm and Carrying On'.

Many drugs are not only poisonous but also addictive in themselves. Cravings are frozen into the ice-ball pattern of hurt caused by the poisoning. Anyone like me who has tried to give up smoking will know how we can love the thing we hate even when we know the damage it is causing us. However, most of us only use these artificial supports to help numb us to painful feelings that haunt us when we don't, even though we are getting fat or wheezing our way to work.

Witness-Trauma

It is a hurt to watch other people being hurt or suffering, especially when you can do little about it. Whether it is your big brother bashing your little brother, or bombs being dropped on people's houses, witnessing these events is painful and needs to be acknowledged as such.

Every day many of us addictively watch the 'News' which is usually a catalogue of people being killed or injured, losing battles or otherwise showing how powerless we are. These 'witness' memories form ice-balls just as much as if they had happened to us. 'Post-Traumatic Stress Disorder' is now a diagnosable 'condition' caused by witnessing horrors, especially in war situations.

One effect of allowing these memories to stay frozen is that our ability to care for others may also get frozen. Witnesses can become numb to the suffering of others. Without understanding the process of accumulating such distresses, people are often accused of being evil, wicked or, heartless. Showing them more suffering in order to try and awake their compassion doesn't work. More ice is formed.

Competition

Our economic system is founded on competition, winners, losers and the phoney idea that we do not have enough resources for everyone. The need to convince us that this is normal, inescapable and beneficial to everyone leads to filling our heads with untruths, including untruths about our human nature.

We are not born with competitive feelings where everyone is a rival to be beaten. We are born with co-operative feelings where everyone is a potential supporter and collaborator. Luckily, this is so deep within our beings that we do act 'altruistically' despite almost everything in society pushing us in the opposite direction, but it is still a struggle to make a 'living' without engaging is the competitive culture ingrained in almost everything.

The oppressive society has to constantly work to keep us convinced of the validity of their lies. Several times a week for example, we are invited to watch television shows such as 'The Great Pottery Throwdown', 'Bake Off' or the 'The Great British Sewing Bee' which not only are based on the concept of 'only one winner' but uses exclusion as a visible punishment for not being fast/clever/ talented enough. We are led to believe this is harmless entertainment but it isn't. It is a dramatized version of everyone's working life, echoed in our political systems. We are meant to find it exciting, but interestingly, the pain the competitors feel when they have to say goodbye to people who have become friends, is palpable. More watchers now tell me they switch over channels for the last few minutes when the names of those to be expelled are announced. They, like me, find it upsetting and a complete distraction from the pleasure gained from watching the craftspeople do their best work.

There seems to be little that the oppressive society does not turn into a competition with awards, money and status for the tiny minority who beat all the others. Likewise, our political system is just like a sport or a war, out to demolish the opponents or enemies. As such it is as much a part of the problem as anything else.

Imagining a world not based on competition is increasingly hard but increasingly necessary. It will start with us melting our own competitive ice-balls and redefining what it means to 'win' or 'lose'.

Hierarchies

Creating hierarchies is a widespread behaviour based on distress patterns with a long historical precedent. Nearly all forms of organisation imposed on each other by humans have been triangular in shape. Slave societies, Kingdoms, Feudalism, Capitalism, Tribalism and many forms of Caste systems all over the world have created tiny numbers of powerful leaders at the top with ever growing layers of subordinates, minions and lower orders descending to the bottom, of a triangular system.

One aspect of hierarchy which comes apparent when the phenomena of the human distress pattern is understood is that it *multiplies* the harm caused by an individual's ice-balls. One extremely distressed individual with an automatic gun in his hands can cause carnage in a school classroom, killing and injuring quite a handful of people before they are stopped, but a person in a position of power over others could find they have access to resources, protection, and authority to inflict their 'patterns' on *thousands* of others.

Even on a more minor scale, e.g. when your best friend is appointed a Prefect at school and you are not – suddenly the power balance in the relationship is altered and the peer relationship vanishes, often along with the mutual trust and respect. Our lives are brimming with these hurtful experiences.

In our current age few of us have experienced anything else. As children we soon learn we are at the bottom of our family hierarchy with almost no rights of our own and in which our parents own and control everything. We go to school and this experience is reinforced by teachers on the basis of age, ability, gender, social class and wealth. We go to work and it is the same. Every organisation you join, every church you attend, every service you use, is organised around a form of hierarchy. In Britain we are born into a Monarchy in which there is one King or Queen and all the rest of us are 'Subjects'. The Royal Family traditionally believe they are the voice of God on Earth as do some political or religious leaders. People – heretics

– who have questioned this have been killed for such views. 'Knowing our place' can seem like the best way to survive.

The experience of true 'peerness' is almost unknown to most of us, except possibly in our informal friendship networks. Even when we make attempts to be 'collective' or set up 'flat' or 'circular' organisational structures, we soon create hierarchies because it is all we know. Talk of 'equality' means little when we are all immersed from day one into the opposite.

There will need to be a lot of ice-ball melting and building of new experiences before we can create new organisational forms in which everyone has an equal and valued role, however different those roles may be.

Powerlessness

Of all the pieces of misinformation we must believe, the idea that we are powerless to change anything has to be the most pervasive. To install this idea in our heads even when there are so many of us wanting change, we have to be starved of any model of people getting together, planning alternatives and creating them themselves. It is not that these things don't happen, it is just that it is not on the news, in the press or even on social media. This is especially true if the people taking matters into their own hands are working class.

Steve Sprung, a working- class film maker made an independent film called 'The Plan'. It chronicled the true story of the men at Lucas Aerospace who were threatened with redundancy from their jobs making Rolls Royce Engines for fighter planes – a market which had 'dried up' with the end of World War 11. They came up with a plan to re-tool their factory to make socially useful products. They designed in detail and were helped to manufacture some such products, generally proving that it could be done.

The Government of the time and its' agencies recognised the viability of their plans but in effect blocked their production. They admitted that they couldn't let it happen because if they were to allow people on the shop floor to control production 'The world would be turned upside down'. Their edifice of lies about working-class people would come tumbling down along with the whole hierarchical infrastructure built to keep them out of power. *(See https://vimeo.com/305253552 for a 30 minute version, or 'www.The Plan That Came From The Bottom Up' for the full length film)*

The world is full of brilliant people like the workers at Lucas Aerospace. You may be one yourself.

The disconnection which comes about through segregation, the division of working people into two classes, one oppressing the other, and the weight of internalised oppression all conspire to stop us feeling our own power. Added to this is the crushing of our imaginations to create alternatives that could work.

When you stand back and catch a glimpse of the relentless onslaught to our sense of power, it is a wonder that we still get out of bed every day. Nonetheless, we can see that Shelley the poet was right when he implored us to

"Rise like Lions after slumber

In unvanquishable number-

Shake your chains to earth like dew

Which in sleep had fallen on you

Ye are many-they are few." — *Percy Bysshe Shelley*.

Powerlessness really is a fraud.

Part Two:

Reclaiming Our Minds

Yes, we can! In fact, we are doing this all the time but without a complete understanding of how we do it. We do kiss and cuddle our children, play with them and reassure them when they are upset. We do the same for our closest partners, friends and relatives, and in maybe a more restrained form to colleagues, acquaintances and even complete strangers.

It helps to remember that **we are always more than just our patterns.** We have parts of our brains fully functioning and able to think rationally, creatively and freshly. Strong emotions are embedded in our human nature – joy, empathy, courage, love, righteous anger, even ecstasy. These remain intact despite every attempt to dehumanize us. We are marvellously resilient.

Looking back over half a century of grappling with this phenomenon, I have come to see two almost distinct areas of work which need to be done in order to realise our full potential. They are like two wings of an aeroplane, both of which are needed in order to fly straight. One is healing and restoration, the other is thinking and planning future actions. Many of us need to do both.

Healing and Restoration

We can and do help each other much more than we are led to believe. This 'knowledge' is in us, like a sparrow knowing how to build a nest without going to 'Nest School'. No one has to teach a baby to cry when they are hungry. We instinctively do many things which help ourselves and each other to 'feel better' when we are hurt, upset or bereaved and collectively these actions have undoubtably prevented us from already blowing the world to smithereens despite having created the means to initiate nuclear holocausts several times over.

As well as confiding in our families and friends, we talk to anyone who appears to be listening (sometimes even if they don't!);

We go to the pub or club and have a good laugh;

We go to our churches, synagogues, temples, mosques and other places of worship to experience community and be reminded of our human values; to sing and pray together;

we seek out socially acceptable forms of emotional release or 'discharge' at social gatherings and arts events - especially comedy;

we organize special events to cry and grieve such as funerals and wakes;

we go to football matches to shout our heads off;

we push ourselves through sweats and shakes to do scary things from performing on stage to bungee jumping;

we watch films which make us laugh or cry;

we join support groups to help rid ourselves of particular patterns eg addictions;

we ask our doctors for counselling (or pay for it ourselves);

we sign up to 'spiritual' communities which practice uninterrupted listening, for example to the holders of a 'talking stick' or another designated object,

We turn to the natural world as a safe place to restore our connection with the world around us;

We organise protests, petitions and campaigns to counter our feelings of powerlessness and isolation.

Most Real Work is Voluntary

The whole concept of 'working people' is misleading, commonly referring to the work we do for money, but much of our real work is additional and/or voluntary. Without this aspect of our labour our societies could not function, and doing this work is helping us not only to survive, but to stay connected to our humanity. Every day for example at least one meal is prepared for almost every person on earth. Every day washing, cooking and cleaning are carried out without payment, usually by women, whether they live in mansions or refugee camps. Even in our more 'modern' societies much of this essential work is taken for granted, undervalued and almost invisible.

The Vital Role of Parenting

Those of us who are fortunate enough to have children already are doing a major job of creating a new generation of people who have as much of their minds intact as we can manage, despite our own un-melted ice-balls. It is the place in which we can love another unconditionally and be our most selfless. Even if we do not actually give birth to the children we can, and do, love and care for them in a multitude of unpaid and paid roles from Grandparents to Teachers. Children's friends are also important resources for their healthy upbringing.

Parenting is still a voluntary role, unfettered by the need to make a profit or please an employer. Parents, or full-time carers, provide the foundation for any child to develop healthily. They also often have to fulfil the role of 'ally', protecting their child from the ravages of oppression as best as they can. No State provider can replace this.

Being able to protect children from all hurts and consequent ice-balls is not possible, but everything we can do to help our children recover is useful. The thing which makes that harder is always our own un-melted ice-balls, so the more we can get them out of the way the better. Allowing our children to feel their feelings, however noisily, is one way in which most of us need a lot of support and encouragement.

Parents are an oppressed group in our own right. The System will try to co-opt our role into one of their agents, bringing up our children to be useful to them – productive, compliant etc. and will heap blame on any one of us who seems to be 'failing'. This can be easily internalised or at worst, turned on the child themselves.

Being a Friend

We have underestimated the role of friendship in a healthy society.

Much of my adult life has been trying to organise the closure of segregated schools for disabled children and to create instead mainstream schools which support natural relationships between all children. This is because the connection between a diverse range of people is the only way we come to understand our commonality and to care about each other. If these relationships are prevented in childhood, we never fully recover. We have 'learned' that we do not need each other, or worse, that we hamper each other's development, whilst in fact the opposite is true.

This applies to all divided peoples, including rich and poor, currently segregated by the Public/Private School System. You only have to look at our fractured and rivalrous adult societies to see the proof.

Friendship is the most enduring relationship we have. It is not 'institutionalised' like a marriage or shaped by laws of inheritance and familial duties like child/parent/sibling relationships. It is freely chosen and freely given with few expectations from 'outside'. Because it is a relationship outside of the law, the significance of it is almost overlooked. This is why it can be so revolutionary in our lives.

Much of the attention we need to at least stay 'sane' i.e. prevent the build-up of ice-balls to such a point we can no longer function, comes within friendships.

This is just as true for children as adults. It is noticeable for example that during the pandemic of 2020/21 when schools were closed for most pupils, the most common phrase coming out of the mouths of said children was "I miss my friends".

Caring for Each Other

Outside the role of paid 'carer' there is a much bigger pool of human activity which includes thousands of small acts of kindness and support for people who need a bit of help. This can be physical or emotional and can range from doing an elderly person's shopping, to manning a lifeboat for the Royal National Lifeboat Institution. Much of it is virtually invisible and taken for granted. Blood donors keep the NHS able to function, and most charitable organisations rely on voluntary Trustees to be allowed to form, but there is virtually no recognition of this and other unpaid work, or that we constantly help to heal each other.

Big Boys do Cry. Adult men have a bit of a harder time using each other in these healing ways because their 'training' is to hide their feelings and compete with each other all the time. Cars and football are acceptable topics of conversation for blokes but not their broken hearts. Nevertheless, they do manage to listen to each other sometimes, have a good laugh together, and even shed some healing tears when circumstances allow. The experience of belonging to the 'Crucible' quickly taught me that men and women have the same capacity to express emotions if they feel safe enough. Some blokes can cry for England, given a chance.

To repeat - the fundamental logic of this insight is that our minds can create ice-balls, but can also melt ice-balls.

It cannot be stated enough times that any society built on the distress patterns of a few requires the installation of distress patterns in the minds of the many, or it just couldn't work. We wouldn't lend ourselves to its continuation:

Without 'Frozen Needs' and addictions we would not create markets for fashion, drugs, cosmetics and a multitude of things we not only don't need, but can actually harm us.

Without patterns of competition, fear of exclusion and false notions of scarcity we would not hide behind national borders or build weapons of war.

Without being able to 'sell' us things there could be no exploitation of labour or natural resources.

Without experiencing isolation as children we could not believe as adults that even though we live amongst several billion other people, we are alone and powerless to organize a better world.

Turning up the Heat

The Power of Touch, our First Language

When we slither into the world our first need is to feel the warm skin of someone else. Our skins are loaded with sensory nerve endings which send messages to our brains about our surroundings, the main message being that we are not alone. We all seem programmed to respond to a new baby by touching, caressing, stroking, cuddling and kissing them. It is how we build connection, bond, bring the new life into the collective warmth of the family who are predisposed to answer her/his needs. Touch is much more necessary than any other sense. A blind/deaf child can still know they are safe and loved if they can feel you.

This however is a life-long need, not just for birthdays. If the 2021 pandemic taught us anything, when we were discouraged from touching each other for fear of passing on the covid virus, it was the agony of physical separation, and the relief of feeling a hug that we remember so vividly. During 'Lock Down' people bought more puppies than before in order to help fill the need to have something warm and alive to touch, and I am equally sure many cats are still purring in their extended role as surrogate humans.

Shaking or holding hands, hugging and kissing is a normal part of most cultures, but out of the context of parenting or marriage, society seems to limit, or discourage this natural instinct. This is especially true in the UK and the USA.

There are a lot of written and unwritten 'rules' about it. You can hug someone when you meet for example, but not for too long. Many of these come from the problematic fact that our distress patterns may often include sexualised feelings and behaviours which are inappropriate. Acting on such patterns can be abusive and protections are needed both from actual abuse and litigation, especially in work places, but at what cost is this to us? How can you measure the harm caused by an absence of comfort?

In the 'Crucible' we wrote our own rules about physical contact. It was recognised first and foremost that holding hands was a crucial step towards stopping someone feeling alone, so any shared time between people in pairs, groups or even large circles began by people linking hands. This would not be seen as 'professional' in most other therapeutic meetings, but soon felt completely natural to us. We knew someone was there with us at last! We did hold people if they needed that extra safety to sob out old memories into our soggy T-shirts, but always with their permission. And goodbye hugs were long, and of mutual comfort as we separated.

It was equally important for our safety in the 'Crucible' that sexual touching or romancing in general was not allowed other than between those who had already formed such a relationship before they joined. It was not a 'Happy Hunting Ground' and nearly everyone understood why and counselled about these sort of feelings instead.

The healing power of touch has been understood and practiced for over 60 years since the 'Crucible' first formed, but we thousands of practitioners have not yet succeeded in 'naturalising' such insights into our daily lives in the 'outside world'. During this time however, scientists have been uncovering evidence that we were right. If you type 'The power of Touch' into an internet search browser, you will be led to many articles about their research. For example, there have been experiments showing that premature babies thrive more when strapped to their mother's chest than isolated in an incubator, or that hugging someone for more than twenty seconds helps release serotonin, the 'happy' hormone into our bloodstreams which can trigger emotional healing.

The June 2022 edition of the 'National Geographic' magazine is dedicated to the subject of touch. On the cover the editors state that *'Research reveals how our connections with others keep us healthy'* and inside the cover is a mine of useful information, well worth reading. However, it is noticeable that whilst much is known about the effects of touch on us, little is still known as to the science behind it. Given however that major research into anything is usually only funded if profits for the funders are likely to be made as a result, perhaps it is not surprising that so little is still known by the scientific community about the power of something we all have already, for free, literally at our fingertips.

In fact, it is worth questioning whether effort is going into *undermining* this knowledge in us, lest we start using it for own purposes. Is this why it is becoming normal to introduce 'No Physical Contact' policies in our workplaces and schools? Is this why we still feel almost afraid of ourselves?

Perhaps searching out the increasing scientific evidence will help us to have the necessary confidence in our own instincts, knowledge and experience around the power of touch. We could fully embrace this power and share it widely. Humanity itself will profit.

The Power of Attention

As well as the power of touch, we have another marvellous gift, also given free by Mother Nature, our attention. Our attention is more than just pointing our eyes and ears at a particular person or thing. It is a decision to take our mind off all other distractions – our to-do lists or our own ice-balls – in order to bring to bear our full minds on something outside of ourselves. In the case of paying a person attention it is listening carefully to what is said, the tone of voice, the posture and body movements. It is holding in mind everything you already know about that person (if anything) and being aware of when different emotions are being felt, for example sadness, anger or embarrassment creeps into their voice or makes them blush.

When we focus our attention in this way something happens in the minds of the person at which it is aimed - **they feel noticed.** They feel someone is there with them and an automatic reaction is set into motion. Almost every ice-ball includes a recording of being alone, because if someone had been paying us attention at the time of the first hurtful experience we would have melted it then and there. No ice-ball would have formed.

Simply touching someone can break their sense of isolation. It is sensory evidence that they are not alone. Whenever it becomes obvious to a person that they are no longer alone it seem to trigger their (our) natural healing process. They giggle with embarrassment, or start talking non-stop. Maybe they get hot and sweaty or tears begin to well up. If we carry on giving the person our attention instead of trying to get them to stuff these emotions back inside, some real healing will take place, and all you had to do was **keep quiet, keep focused and look pleased.** If this is all you do it will be part of a revolution. A revolution of the mind. A reclaiming of our ability to think flexibly, to be creative and to have a clearer picture of reality.

There is more we can do if we recognize the power of this process and start to structure it into our lives.

Learning to Take Turns

Talking to someone who is listening is one of the main ways we start to process information or examine some 'frozen' memories. To help this process we could **stop interrupting** each other, desperately trying to bring the attention back to our particular ice-balls. Instead we could **take turns**. We could do this covertly – without making it obvious - by inner monitoring of more equally balanced conversation, or we could make it obvious, bring out a timer and suggest a five-minute each exchange of talking and listening (sometimes called a 'mini-session'). I have tried these many times in training workshops on Inclusion, and at meetings of all sorts. It takes a surprising amount of nerve to structure what is usually a 'free-for-all' but it never fails. Many people reported this experience as being a 'first' in their life, in both roles.

In the 'Crucible' it was usual to exchange a whole hour each. This precious time we called a 'Session'. Additional agreements were made to help make these sessions safe and useful, the most important of which was confidentiality – we never repeated what was shared in a session, then or ever, and not even with the person who shared it.

All this was formal and structured but through the experience we became aware that in everyday life we are all trying to have 'sessions', often simultaneously! We became somewhat skilful at recognizing the difference between an attempt to have a session and a conversation which is an exchange of current ideas, thinking or information. "I just need to rant about something" or "Can you listen whilst I cry about my dead cat" are leading to a 'session'. "I've got an idea as to how to mend your tap" or "Have you notice the buds on the cherry tree?" are not sessions. These two types of conversation require two different types of response. The first mostly to shut up and listen without much comment, and the second to engage with in an appropriate way.

Our Attention is Limitless

"It's just like a Magic Penny,

Hold it tight and you won't keep any,

Lend it, spend it, you'll have so many,

They'll roll all over the floor"

The Magic Penny – Malvina Reynolds

Malvina was singing about love, but she could well have been singing about attention – maybe because they are aspects of the same thing. Like love, we need not be afraid of running out of it. However, lending and spending our attention requires effort and focus, which is made harder by our own unmet needs for attention. Because we have to batter down the pull of our own 'ice-balls' to get into the melting warmth of someone else's eyes and ears, it can feel tiring to keep listening. We can genuinely run out of the energy required at the time to do this, but our attention will later replenish itself. Our supply is in fact infinite, just like our ability to love. However, understanding that we cannot always be available is important.

Most people who have not experienced a structured sort of listening time are not aware that they are demanding attention without permission. Giving attention is 'work' which can require surprising amounts of energy. This is a reason to keep noticing – or even asking – if the listener wants to listen just then, and to make sure it is reciprocated as much as possible, then or later.

It is easier when we know the session is time-limited, so we could all carry little kitchen timers in our pockets which are brought out when we feel it could be useful. "Tell you what, I've only got ten minutes just now. How about we share it, five each? I'll time it…" You will find that just a few minutes uninterrupted time feels quite long and much more useful than the usual battle for attention in which neither of you gets to the end of the story.

Those amongst us who are most unaware of our habits of hogging the attention are often avoided or not invited which of course makes us more desperate to find that 'safe space' in which to talk a lot. Those of us who are more on the compulsive listener side of things may crave solitude to avoid exploitation, despite having painful feelings of isolation. Taking turns can help all this. There is no reason why this could not become a 'normal' part of our culture as human beings.

Speeding Things Up

Many of the suggestions in this book could be used at any time in ordinary life without setting up a structured relationship. You can do it over a cup of tea and a chat. However, some of you may want to be more focussed and intentional in using your attention to directly help someone in their ice-ball-melting process. There are some tools we can all learn which might be useful, especially within an agreed time-frame or 'session'.

Melting Small Ice-Balls (Intermittent Patterns)

Given that we are all of us trying to melt the ice-balls we know we have, a 'normal' conversation is often no more than two people competing for each other's attention. Learning to **stop interrupting** can in itself take quite a lot of practice and will-power. Once we can do that for sufficient lengths of time we can let some words out of our mouths, to ask open questions or offer a 'contradiction'.

Something worth understanding about patterns is that there is **no point trying to argue with them.**

An ice-ball is not intelligent. It is a rigid recording, like a DVD of an Alfred Hitchcock horror film. To 'contradict' a pattern is not an invitation to try and demolish it by your stunning logic or superior intellect. Most people just wait for you to stop talking until they can play their recordings again. You have to drill down to the roots of their proposition and really listen to the inevitable hurtful experiences that caused them to start building that particular ice-ball.

Contradictions and Directions

Many ice-balls include a recording which sounds like a malevolent intruder in your head. They often sound uncannily like your Mum on a bad day, or a teacher at school who thought you were a waste of space.

A **'contradiction'** is anything which will help the focus person recognize that their ice-ball, is a past memory and not present time reality. When we have listened enough to the person's story and made some sort of guess as to the detailed contents of someone's ice-ball, we can try to create an action, or phrase which is completely contradictory to this content. We can model it ourselves, or ask the person to model it for themselves. When we get this contradiction right, we are rewarded by an automatic 'melting' which shows itself in some emotional response, a roar of laughter perhaps, or eyes brimming with tears. The person might get hot, flush or shudder. They might suddenly give you a lot more information which they may well have only just remembered.

The notion of illness, disease and madness have made us afraid of our own strong emotions and their expression. We try and therefore stop these feelings, mistaking them for the distress itself rather than the healing of the pain through a perfectly natural process. This is especially true of crying loudly, or raging but there is nothing to really fear. It is just noise. It doesn't mean the person has 'broken down' or lost control of themselves and will smash your house up, or that you might need to call the police or an ambulance, When the timer beeps at the end of an agreed exchange of attention, they will just stop, get their attention back into the present, and thank you for listening.

Asking someone what the current difficulties **remind** them of, asking them to recount their earliest memory of something similar and, if any form of emotion starts to well up, asking them to tell the story **again** will extend the usefulness of the 'session'.

There is no end to the contradictions we can dream up. With practice you can try to formulate in your own head what false message you think forms the content of the ice-balls being explored, or triggered. You can then formulate a different, possibly the opposite message including tone of voice and body language and then model it yourself. For example, if someone's recording says "I am not very clever" you could stand up straight, and with a beaming face say "I am bright as a button!" You could invite them to copy you. They will find it impossible to do this without giggling or something like it as the nature of a distress recording is to be rigid and repetitive.

The more fine-tuned you can design these 'contradictions' the better they will work. Your first attempt may not work but amazingly the focus person will usually give you some more information, "Actually it's more like blah blah" and you can then re-form your contradiction until you create one which works.

A contradiction does not have to be the 'truth', it just has to be sufficiently different to the recording to elicit some sort of emotional response. You could ask someone to repeat something they have said repeatedly in a flat tone without apparently feeling anything – replaying the recording – and ask them to say the same thing in a high squeaky voice. Even just thinking about doing this will probably make them laugh. Or again, you could do it for them. The laughter is the melting happening before your eyes.

A '**direction**' is a certain type of contradiction which is based on rational thinking as opposed to the contents of the focus person's distress recordings. A direction is a few words which should guide our actions despite what we 'feel'. Sometimes we have to write these things down and stick them to our fridge doors because our 'feelings' are always trying to convince us otherwise. We might have to be reminded that we do not have to eat that cream-filled piece of chocolate cake however much we want to.

Appreciation

Reminding someone of their true natures, gifts, qualities, powers as separate and independent of their distress recordings is almost always useful. Many other self-help or therapeutic bodies use 'affirmations' or such like to help people overcome negative feelings about themselves and of course friends and lovers do it all the time. That is why we keep old birthday cards and other such reminders that people love and appreciate us.

Melting Permanent (Chronic) Ice Balls

Chronic physical pain is identified by doctors as pain which continues after the injury has healed. An amputated limb can continue to 'hurt' even when it is not there. Chronic emotional pain is the same.

Chronic Ice-balls, or patterns need a different approach to intermittent patterns. The challenge is firstly to identify the source of the hurt, the early memory which was real, but then to help someone to get their attention off such recordings onto something more real now - 'The War is over and bombs are no longer dropping' for example. The problem is the focus person is usually unaware that they have such recordings and feels like it is just them, just how things are. They/we can become very defensive or scared if you suggest otherwise, but it is always worth ploughing on.

What we are doing is attempting to help the person inside the pattern to get a glimpse of the fact that whilst the first injury was real, it left a recording which is not current reality - not their intelligence working - but which still sounds and feels real. The owners of chronic patterns such as these tend to see the evidence to support their painful emotions all over the place, but will have difficulty noticing, or feeling, evidence that contradicts the monster inside even when such evidence is plentiful.

Anything which helps someone to see that the recording isn't real now but a set of painful memories from the past will help them to not let it completely drive their current behaviour. If we *only* keep their focus on the content of the recording we risk simply reinforcing it by giving it another run, deepening the groove in their neural pathways.

Doing almost anything else will be useful e.g. describing aloud our surroundings now, noticing we are not alone at this minute, cataloguing evidence that actual reality is different to our recorded 'realities' and if we are lucky, being offered a phrase to say which will give us the perspective we need to process the painful emotions locked into the ice-ball which can then start to 'melt'.

Gradually the 'chronic' nature of the pattern will be down-graded to an intermittent pattern by which time we will be able to bring to bear much more of our real intelligence to side-line or overcome it even though it might still be like Winston Churchill's 'Black Dog' waiting in the background to pounce when we let down our guard. *(Black Dog was the name he gave to his intermittent bouts of depression)*.

Alone we will not be able to help everybody. Some chronic patterns can be very dangerous and people saddled with them may have to be physically prevented from acting them out. We do not yet however have a system fit for purpose in this area, as the criminal justice system, and even parts of the mental health system, are founded on the principles of punishment and revenge, not ice-melting. When the phenomenon of the human distress pattern is understood, we will create something much better, or even prevent such terrible patterns being formed in the first place.

However massive our chronic pattern may seem they **never** colonise the whole of our minds. In fact, we can keep 'growing' our minds by stimulating the growth of new neural pathways and new connections until the day we die. Learning a language or taking up a new hobby are all useful ways of keeping our brains functioning and our humanity intact.

Why Bother?

Setting out to deliberately melt your own or other people's ice-balls is no quick-fix therapy. In fact, to be completely honest, it may not even make you feel better to begin with. 'Melting' frozen feelings may be experienced as an 'un-numbing' of pain which you had been trying to forget. The benefits however are literally priceless. Every giggle, every tear- drop, every tremble and every intense word will release a little piece of the real you. As the effect of these expressions accumulate you will notice that other people cannot upset you so easily, that you make better decisions, that the world seems more benign, that you are less driven, less defensive, less confused. You may notice your high blood pressure going down or that you are able to sleep better. You may become conscious of your own ability to not act on feelings you know to be rooted in past distress but to act on your best thinking instead. You will have more attention for other people and for worthwhile activities outside of your 'comfort zone'.

As for giving attention to others, what is more gratifying than being able to give someone their life back? Maybe not all at once, but in precious little parcels. To facilitate someone to gradually reclaim their minds is surely to give them the best gift possible.

We do not have models of people with no distress at all, so the potential of spreading the ability to consciously engage our innate powers of touch, attention and imagination is unknown but hugely promising.

Of the many thousands of people who have already been using these powers with each other, most would say they became better parents, better friends and partners, led more stable lives with less addictions and self-destructive behaviours. The understandings forged between groups of people struggling to recover from the wounds of oppression and internalised oppression have resulted in a real-life education unique in its depth and insight. It has created many thousands of allies working together with the victims of oppression to challenge and end such damaging beliefs and behaviours.

Any form of organising goes better when there is some form of structured listening and room for emotional healing. It is as important as the thinking and planning aspect of the work.

It is impossible to say what impact on the world in general the efforts of people who have had access to the information I have tried to summarise in this book has made, or will make in the future, but it seems clear to me that it is well worth the effort necessary to find out.

SIGHTS

SOUNDS

TIC TOC

SMELLS

TOUCH

TASTES

Information comes in through all our senses. We compare it to everything that we already know, and contrast it to everything we know. Then we 'file' it away so that we can use it when we need to.

When information is processed like this we can use it to create a fresh new response to every situation we are in.

However, when we are hurt, physically or emotionally, we cannot process information in this way. Our minds temporarily stop working, although information is still pouring in through our senses, making a complete recording of the event

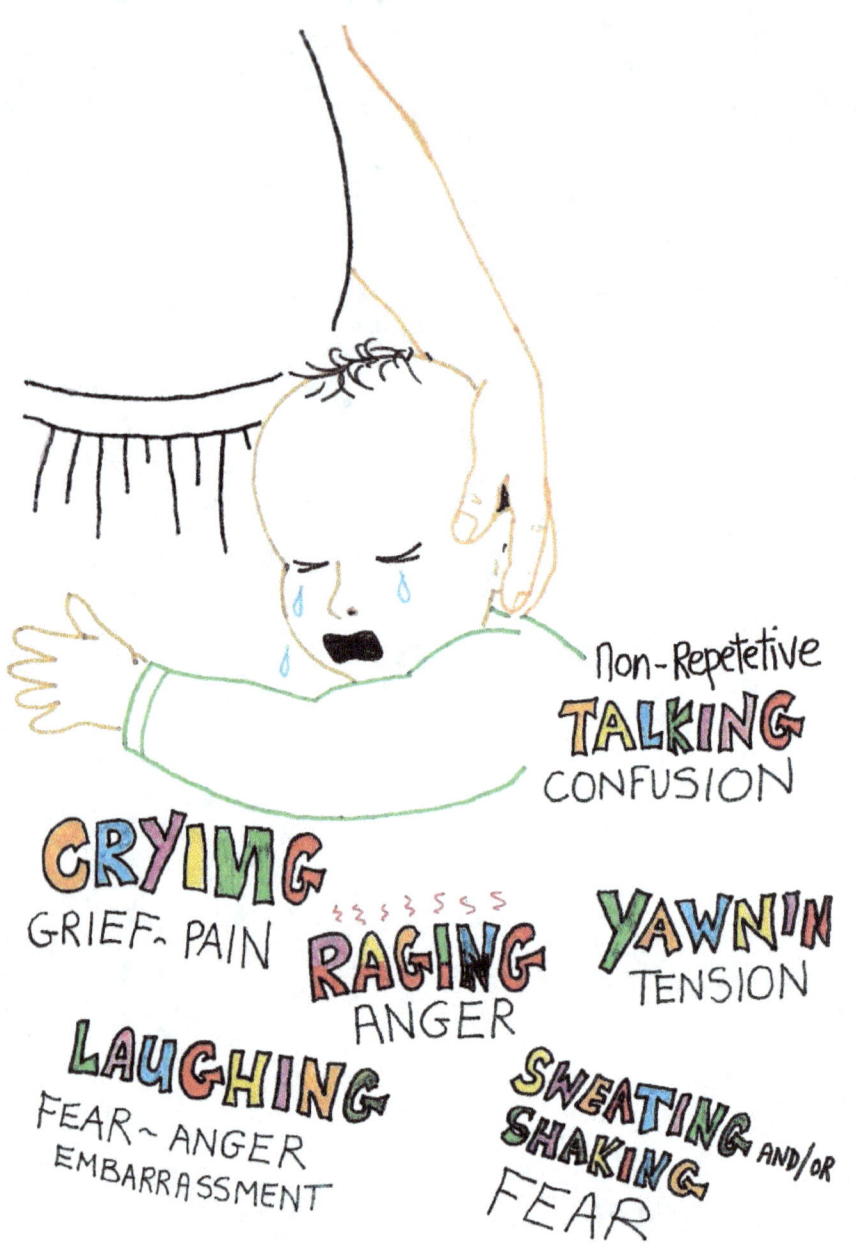

Non-Repetetive
TALKING
CONFUSION

CRYING
GRIEF~ PAIN

RAGING
ANGER

YAWN'N
TENSION

LAUGHING
FEAR~ ANGER
EMBARRASSMENT

SWEATING AND/OR
SHAKING
FEAR

We instinctively try to find a safe person and, if they will allow it, we start to heal ourselves of the hurt by crying, or one of the other physical processes we naturally use to get over the distressing event. If this happens, the information recorded in the painful event becomes just like all the othe information we have. It becomes no more than a useful memory.

If we are not allowed to complete this healing process, the information remains in the form of a recording which includes how we felt at the time. The next time something happens which is *similar enough* to the first time, the recording seems to play and we start to feel and behave how we did the frist time. Our minds temporarily shut down again, and we try to find a safe place to heal the hurt. If we cannot do this, a second recording is added to the first. It becomes like a snowball.

In time our minds become a mixture of useful information and distress recordings which have not been allowed to be processed, or healed. This uses up increasing amounts of our free intelligence, and sometimes makes us feel and behave in ways which are irrational.

This is any two people meeting. We see each other through a distorting bubble of our distress. Not only that, we see the other person's distress before we see them. We do not see things as they really are.

Luckily, it is never too late to process our recorded memories and to reclaim our complete intelligence and freedom of action. All we need is the warm attention of another human being. Most 'normal' interactions between people are two people trying to get the other person to listen to them so that the process can start.

Part Three

Thinking And Planning

As I write this (2022) there seems to be a more general uncovering of the role of oppression and internalized oppression in the perpetuation of inequality including The 'Me Too' movement exposing the continued sexual oppression of women; the 'Black Lives Matter' movement exposing the continued oppression of black people; the Disability Movement exposing the oppression of people with impairments and the Eugenicist programme still operating ; 'Extinction Rebellion' exposing the life-threatening nature of class-based exploitation and greed on the natural world, and Catholics uncovering the cruelty their nuns perpetrated upon unmarried mothers and children in their 'care.

Everywhere these hidden histories are forcing their way into the light of day where they can be examined and defused. In the 1950s when I grew up men didn't cry. Now, you can see big blokes weeping almost every day on the TV. The 'macho' patterns of shame have been dissolved. A young disabled woman, Greta Thunberg, has become a world leader in tackling Climate Change. A black woman has become the first Vice-President of the USA – arguably the most racist nation in the world. The Covid Pandemic has created hard evidence of inequality by recognising our 'key workers' in ways which no one has been able to ignore. The unchallenged power of the billionaire-owned media has become the focus of the 'socialists' fighting for a classless society. We did that! When we decide to engage our rational minds on such barriers, we will eventually break through them.

No individual has brought about this 'uprising'. It has happened because the collective 'consciousness' now allows it, through millions of instances of our own initiatives joining together to change our culture. Social media has perhaps allowed an acceleration of this movement.

Despite all this, there is still a danger. Without sufficient melting of our ice-balls, we are compelled to re-create what we already know, complete with all its mistakes, in every new situation we find ourselves. Even if we were to be parachuted into Nirvana, if still half frozen, we will soon be setting up hierarchies, lusting after the wrong people, excluding people we cannot get along with and so on. It seems important to be aware of this danger right from the start of any new collaborative venture. We need to gradually create new forms of structures which will both facilitate the melting process, and facilitate the planning and building process.

We also need to facilitate the melting and thinking processes of people in the structures which *already* exist to help bring about a change of culture within them.

Protest Is Not Enough

Organizing on the basis of painful emotion is limited in its' effectiveness, yet it is evidently the case that most protests and uprisings have been, and are still, based on anger, rage, fear or indignation, but somehow, even after much bloodshed and supposed reforms the balance of power in the world never changes. The wealth, power and control continue to be sucked up by a tiny minority whilst the huge majority of us carry on giving it to them. The system itself never dies.

To reiterate, a pattern is not intelligent. It is no more than a recording of the past charged with painful emotion which masquerades as current reality. Most of our protests and campaigns are aimed to stop something 'bad' happening. We are against things that hurt us, but **what are we for?**

We need to learn a whole host of new skills, and create a new infrastructure in which to put these skills to the genuine service of our humanity and the natural world.

Formulating Good Questions

The point of a good question is to help people to think about something in a way they might not have before. They are most useful when they by-pass an intellectual analysis of a subject and instead get the person to reflect on their own, lived experience. For example, asking someone what they think about the Governments' education policy is a very different question to "How was school for you?". Formulating good questions, asking them and paying attention to the person trying to think about the answer is something we can all do anywhere. One friend of mine when paying at the till for some purchase or other tried an experiment of asking the shopworker "Is this a kind place to work?". The startled person usually said "No" and then gave my friend a load of information about why. My friend at the time was himself deeply concerned about the dehumanizing of 'work', so he was very happy to listen.

Adam Kay in his book about his time working as a hospital Doctor for the NHS 'This Will Hurt' ended the book which as well as being very funny had told his harrowing story behind his resignation, with a plea to us all "Ask us how our day has been". He believes this simple giving of attention would allow many people like him enough healing that they wouldn't break down themselves or feel they have to leave the profession.

Another friend used her membership of the U3A (University of the Third Age) to invite men who had lived through a War as soldiers to come together to share their memories. In a 'lightly' structured series of meetings the men were invited to talk about, and sometime cry about, painful memories which they had felt they couldn't share for many years.

In my own work with parents of disabled children, our first question was always "What do you love about your child?". Over and over again, through the tears, parents said they had never been asked that question before (the focus had always been on the problems they faced). We helped them to make posters with photos of their child and their own words in answer to the question. This not only changed their position on the battles ahead from victim to ally, but it gave their children a positive reminder that they were not in themselves the problem.

In my work as a Disability Equality Trainer I often asked people to talk about their own impairments, or those of people close to them. *(This only worked within strict guidelines of confidentiality because many disabled people hide their impairments, especially at work, for fear of discrimination.)* Following the initial common reaction of "I don't have any impairments and I don't know anyone who does" gradually the truth seeped out "Well actually I can't hear very well and lip read most of the time..." "I am diabetic and lock myself in the toilet at work to inject my insulin..." "I take medication for depression..." "My sister is in a wheelchair but I don't count her..." "My auntie is in a home for people with learning difficulties but we don't talk about that…" so on and so on. Without the question the course attendees would never have understood that disabled people are not a race apart but ordinary people like, and often including, themselves.

In other areas of my life I have helped facilitate all sorts of timed question and answer sessions "What impact has Capitalism had on your life?" "What led you to become an activist?" "Who is/are your leaders and why?" Any of these questions will bring up feelings for the person asked. This is great, and part of why they work. Talking itself, the odd giggle, yawn, shiver or tear drop that spontaneously pops out during this little space you have created will be a visible sign of someone's ice-ball melting. They will leave that experience with a little more of their intelligence freed to work.

Activists and evangelists from all political parties and religions waste huge amounts of time and effort trying to 'talk' people into changing their political or spiritual beliefs. They would do much better by asking them good questions and listening to the answers.

Making Action Plans

In his book 'Slowdown' (2020) Danny Dorling, whilst trying to explain that *less* economic growth is good for us, proposes that "People find it easier to imagine the end of the world than the end of capitalism". This is probably horribly true, but it doesn't mean we can't.

The Power of Imagination

When nothing exists to meet a need we perceive - not a gadget, a service, a building, a law or an organisation, we have another marvellous gift to bring to bear – our imaginations.

An ice-ball cannot imagine anything it has not already experienced because it is no more than a frozen memory, but the free part of our minds, not paralysed by distress *can*. They are the parts of our minds we use to learn new things, write songs, design a crochet shawl, solve day-to-day problems, answer a good question.

We also do not have to do it alone. Sometimes we need the support of others to help what may feel like coaxing a rusty cog in our brains to start turning. One example of this I have experienced has been through my involvement with the struggle of people with intellectual impairments to be heard. Together with their allies, they have helped to articulate and design completely new ways to organise their lives. These have been called the 'Tools of Inclusion':

It began In Canada in the 1990s when a small group of allies to people with 'severe' impairments invented two processes called MAPs and PATHs ('Making Action Plans' and Planning Alternative Tomorrows with Hope'). They were specifically designed to facilitate people who had been institutionalized to imagine, and then create the kind of life they really wanted, in which they would be supported to have a meaningful life on their own terms.

The process starts with the focus person describing his/her 'dream' life of the future. What would it look like, smell like, feel like – who would be in it, where would they be, what would the person be doing in it? Heavily oppressed people are often good at this because their lives are usually such shit that it isn't hard to imagine it being better.

Once the dream goal has been mapped out, the path to get there is worked out in steps, or stages. These steps always include recognizing the supports already in your life, including people, financial resources and services. Then you look at who else will need to be drawn in to fill the gaps in expertise, resources and gate-keeping powers. Then all the steps are lightly sketched out including the very first step. "What shall we do tomorrow?" - "Phone John and invite him to the next meeting"

Probably no-one has yet reached their Big Dream, the ''North Star' vision but the process has succeeded in creating a direction forward for many people who were destined to remain exactly where they had been 'placed' until the day they died.

Greta Thunberg constantly warns us that this scenario applies to the whole world population 'frozen' into behaviours which are bringing about our own extinction. We need a PATH out and it can begin just by asking "What does the world you want look like?" PATHS need to be created so we move together in the right direction.

The Immediate Task Ahead

The need to think for ourselves is a human need, as necessary as food and shelter. The processes I have described in this little book, healing and planning, require something of which we seem to be in very short supply. **Space.** Space to meet, space to listen and be heard without interruption, space to express our feelings, space to be private, space to make plans.

Where has all the space gone? Homes we rent or buy are designed to be smaller and more crowded than in the past; meeting rooms too expensive, timetables at work too tight. Can we create local, accessible **'Thinking Spaces'** in which both wings of our aeroplane can be developed?

The need to facilitate both the healing and the planning requires many **facilitators.** These are people who have enough attention that they can listen to others, formulate good questions and 'hold' the safe structure of the meeting. Many of them exist already, and many more could be trained.

Can these people identify themselves and come forward to organise around a common programme of social activism that actually works? Can we support them enough that their own ice-balls, or 'patterns', won't get in their way?

Crowdfunding, self-publishing, voluntary organising, online petitions are the beginnings of a new **infrastructure** to fund and build our own alternatives. How can we develop more of this infrastructure so more of our ideas can come to fruition?

"What really matters are the countless small actions of nameless people which create the basis for events which enter history. They always have and they always will."

Howard Zinn/Noam Chomsky - 'Requiem for the American Dream 2015'.

If you want to find ways to apply your own thinking to these tasks, contact me: www.michelinemason.co.uk or email sparrowhawk@mail. com

Guidelines for Facilitating a Listening Circle.

We all need a safe space in our lives in which we can think and feel without fear of criticism or judgement. A Listening Circle is one way to provide this. It is very simple to organise and need cost nothing. Many of you will be amazed at how the structure adds a level of safety which many people have never experienced, and which seems to enable our minds to work better than usual.

Such groups can serve many purposes from problem solving at work or exploring personal difficulties such as addictions. Some people use these groups to start to tell their life stories through which they often reach a greater personal understanding and pride in themselves. Some groups are 'one-offs,' and some meet with the same people regularly for weeks or even years.

They will only work if the ground rules are followed. The facilitator needs to take charge and create the structure which will enable true listening to happen. She/he will need a hand-held timer and will need to get a verbal agreement from each participant on the following three guidelines:

Ground Rules

- Confidentiality: What is said in each persons' time is completely confidential. No one refers to it again, ever, except the person themselves - if they want to.
- Equal Time: everyone has an equal amount of time during which no one interrupts or comments on what they are saying. Listeners maintain an attitude of respect, interest and delight.
- Expressions of emotion such as laughing or crying are welcome if they arise naturally. (Maybe bring a box of tissues to the meeting).

Creating the Structure:

Invite no more than eight people*.

Decide on a place to meet which must be private, usually someone's home, but it could be a room at work or even in a break-out room at a conference or workshop.

Encourage people to be punctual or early. People joining a group which has already started can be very disruptive.

You may or may not offer refreshments before the meeting, but make water available to all.

Sit in a circle as close as you can. If you are comfortable with it, holding someone's hand when taking your turn can add to the safety.

Ask people to begin with something that has gone well in their lives lately or something they are pleased with. Share their pleasure but do not start a conversation about it.

Divide the remaining time equally amongst the number of people present, leaving ten minutes at the end to close the circle.

The facilitator holds the timer (kitchen timers are good) and asks a question for everyone to answer in turn. This must require an answer which is open (there is no 'right' answer), personal and not general. Below are some examples of questions which have already worked well, but there is no end to these.

Set the timer and go round the room. Everyone gives their undivided attention to each person in turn including the facilitator (who is a peer – not an expert). The facilitator thanks each person when the timer goes off and moves the attention of the group to the next person.

Closing the Circle

Use the last ten minutes of your meeting to let each person say something to which they are looking forward. Goodbye hugs are great but should never be forced on people.

It can be tempting to hang round after such a meeting, eat cake and slide into bringing up things which need to remain confidential. Also sticking to a set, agreed time may encourage more future commitments to come to meetings.

This process can work with bigger groups but these would require more people who can facilitate the circles. These larger groups would need to divide into two or more smaller groups with a facilitator in each. This is because real attention is hard to maintain for longer than an hour or so.

Some questions used in various groups:

- What work is meaningful to you?

- Who has been your ally and what makes them so?

- How has racism/sexism/ableism/classism/adultism (pick one!) impacted on your life?

- What was your first connection to nature?

- What makes you feel included?

- What made you decide to be an activist?

If you need some assistance thinking of the right question for the group, please email me at sparrowhawk@mail.com and I will try and suggest some.

GOOD LUCK!

www.ingramcontent.com/pod-product-compliance
Lightning Source LLC
Chambersburg PA
CBHW070941120626
46546CB00004B/1517